I0465814

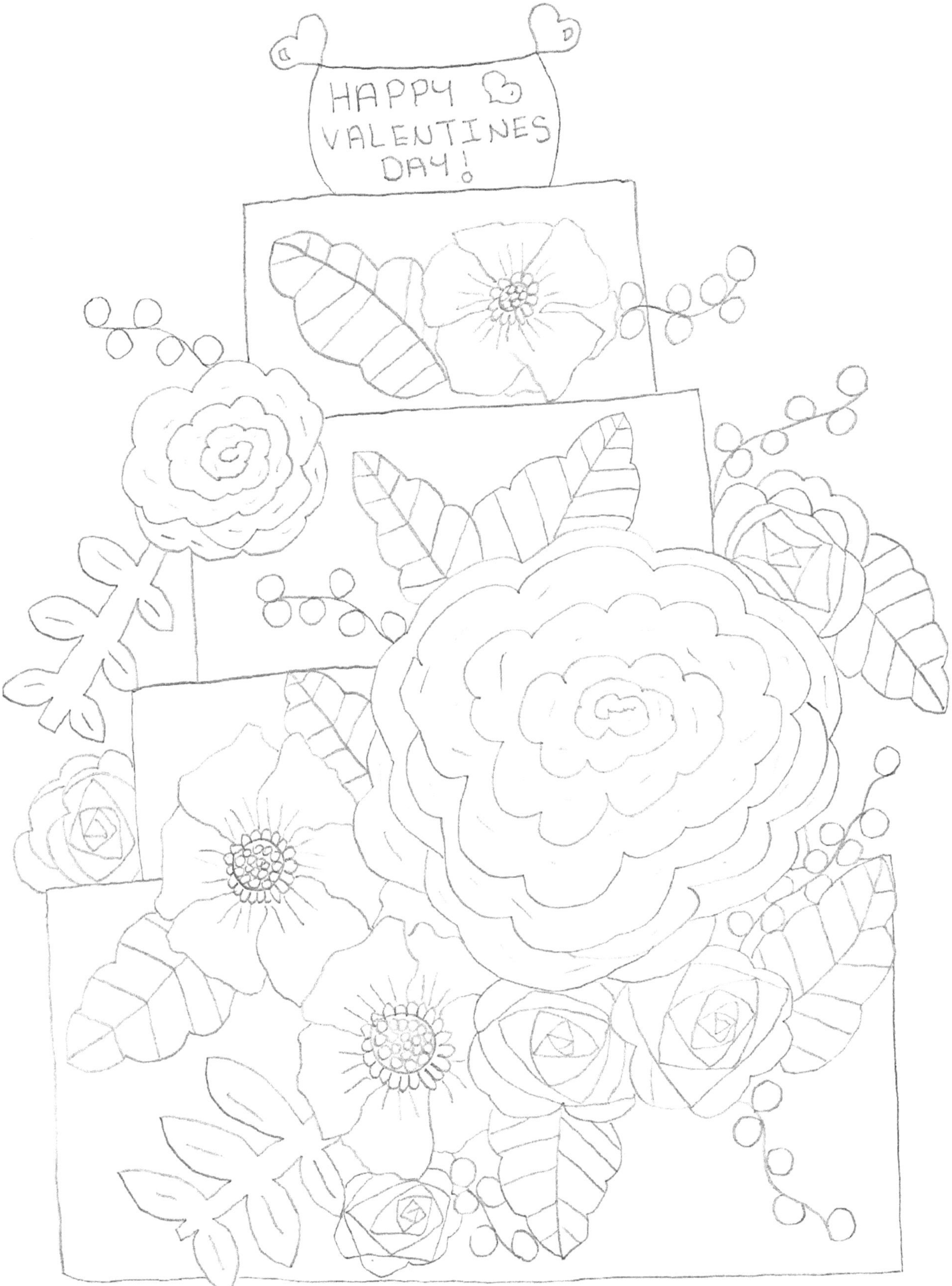

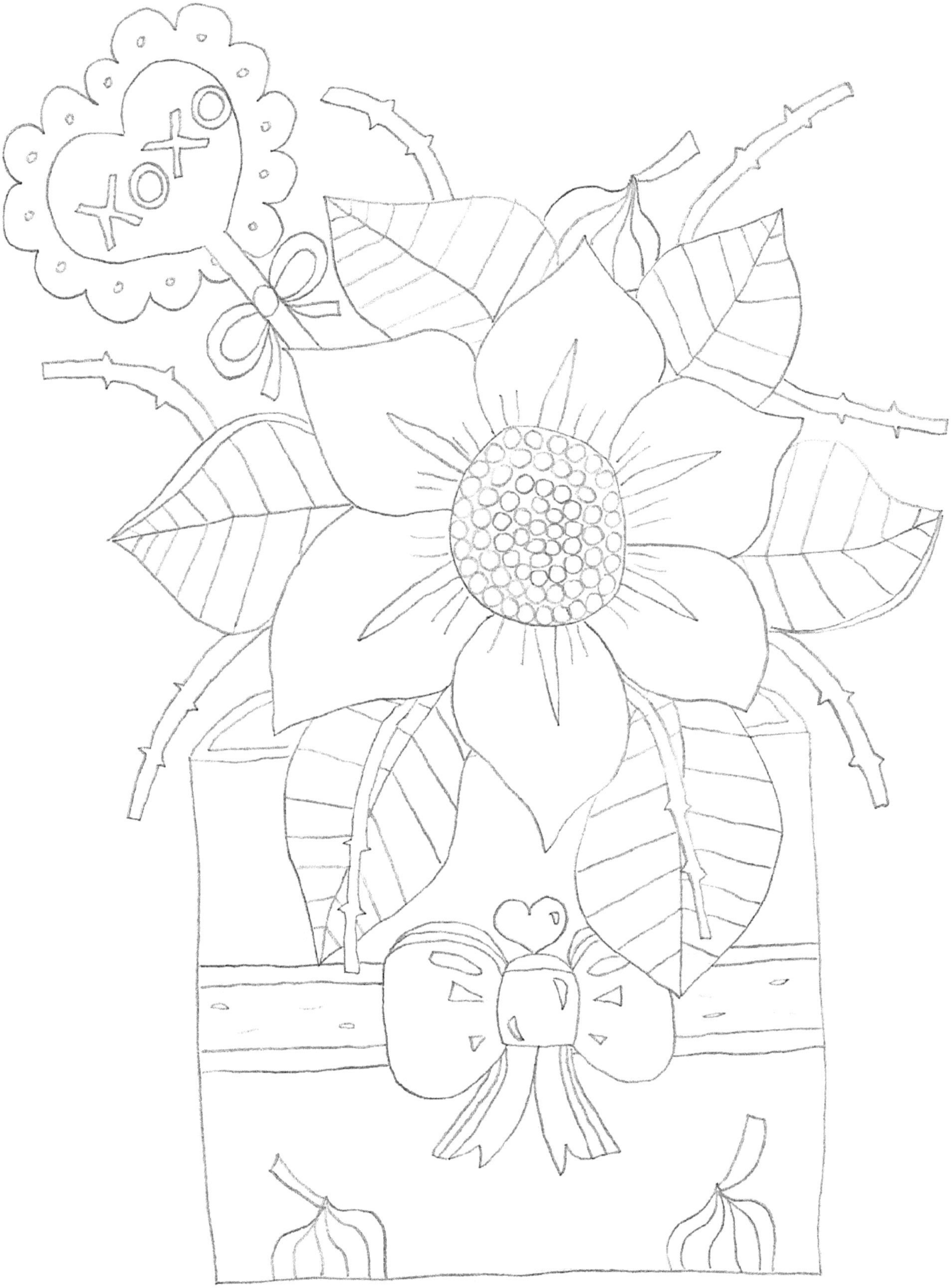
XOXO

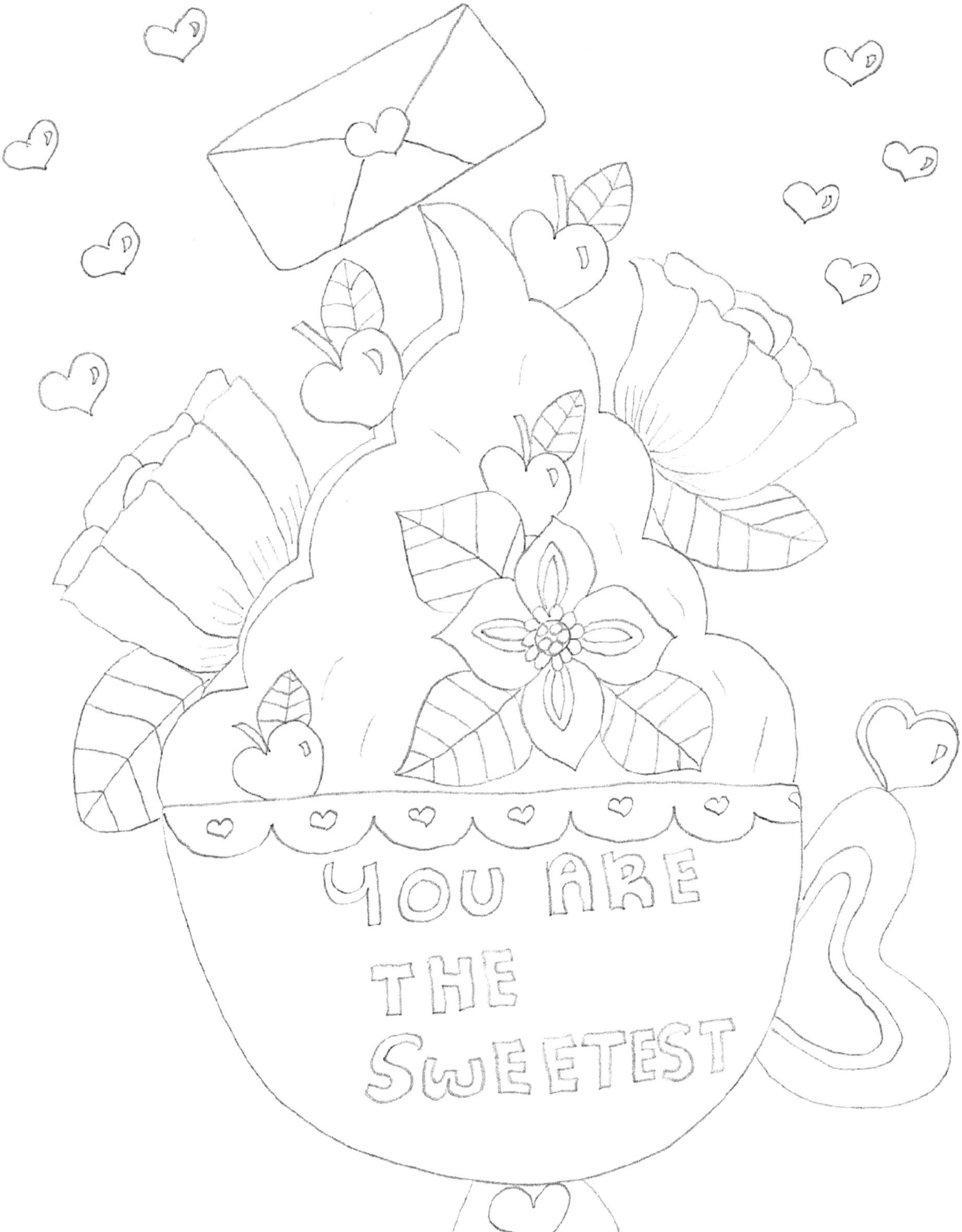
YOU ARE
THE
SWEETEST

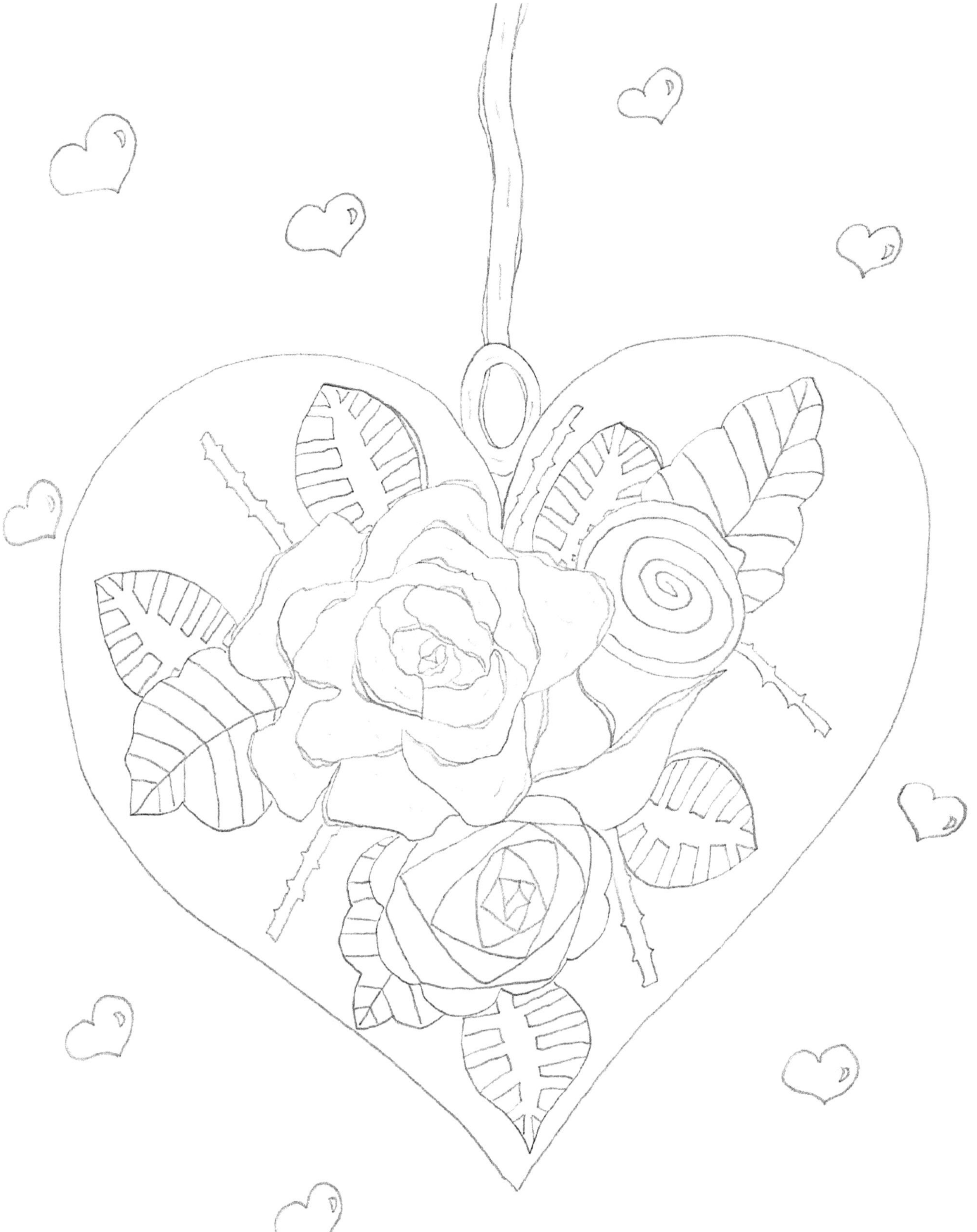

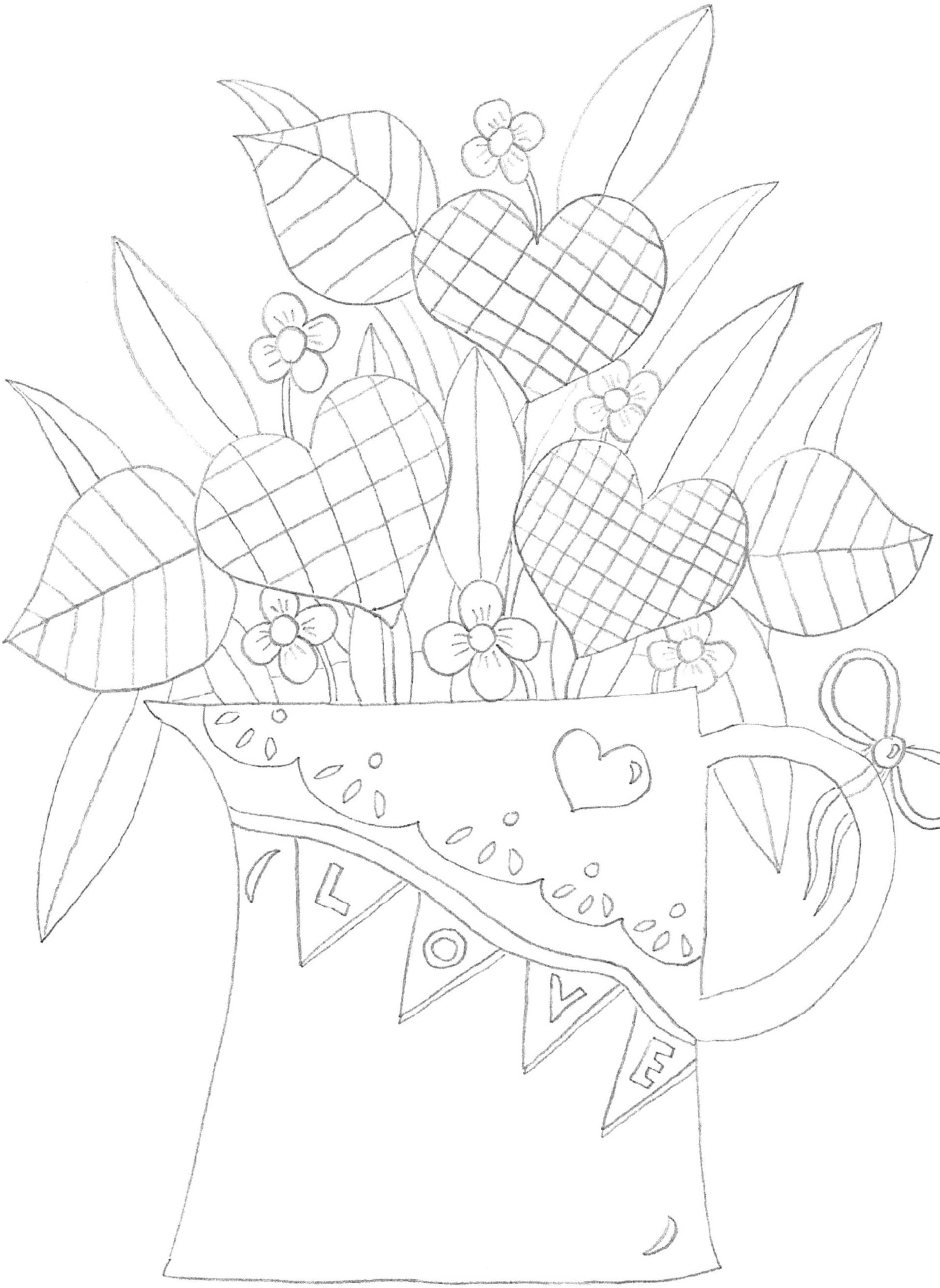
LOVE

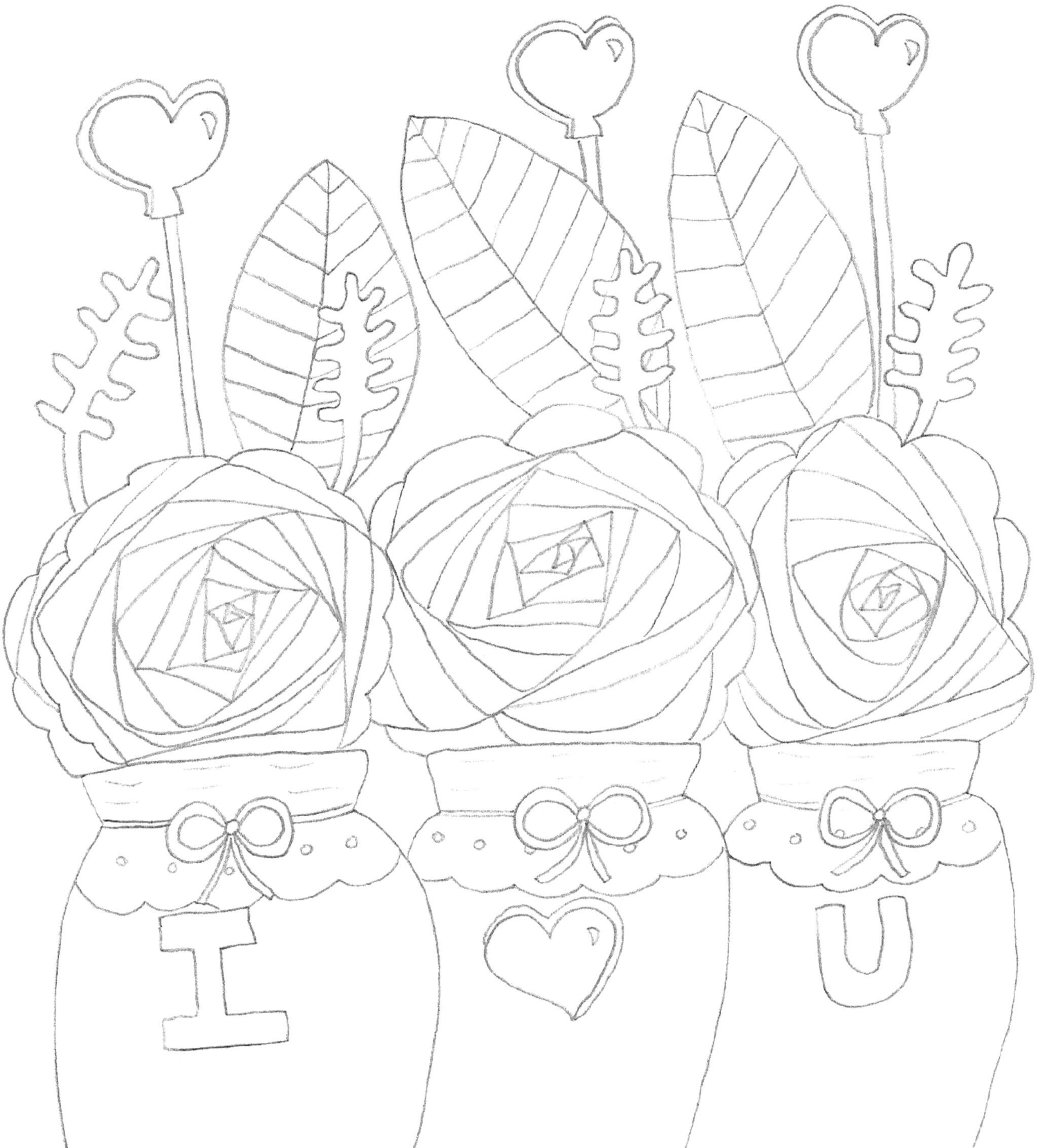
I
U

12
1
2
3
4
5
6
7
8
9
10
11

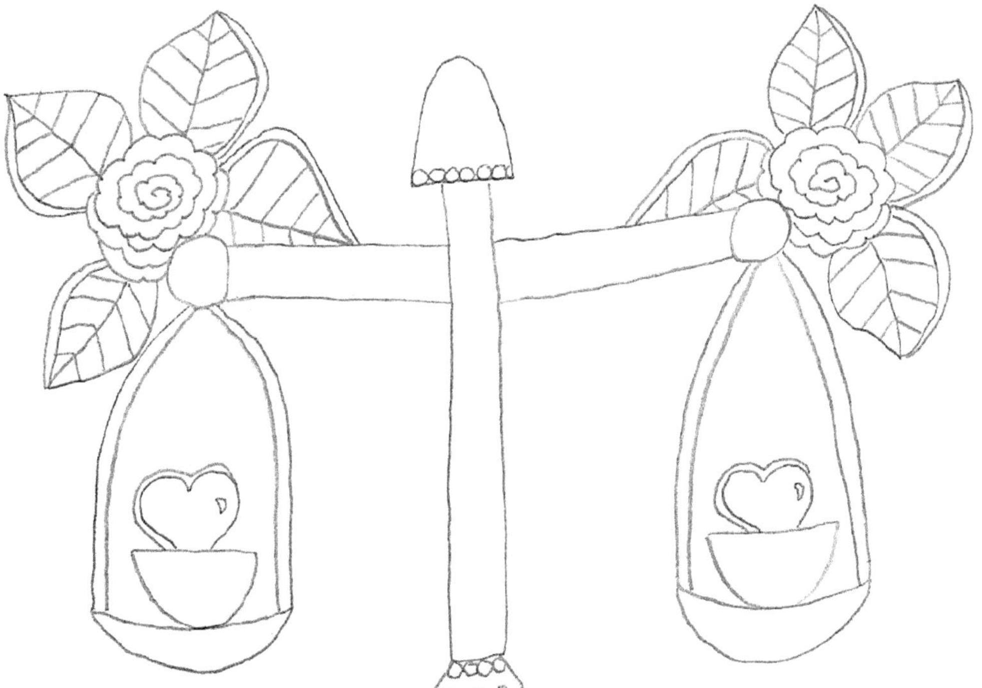

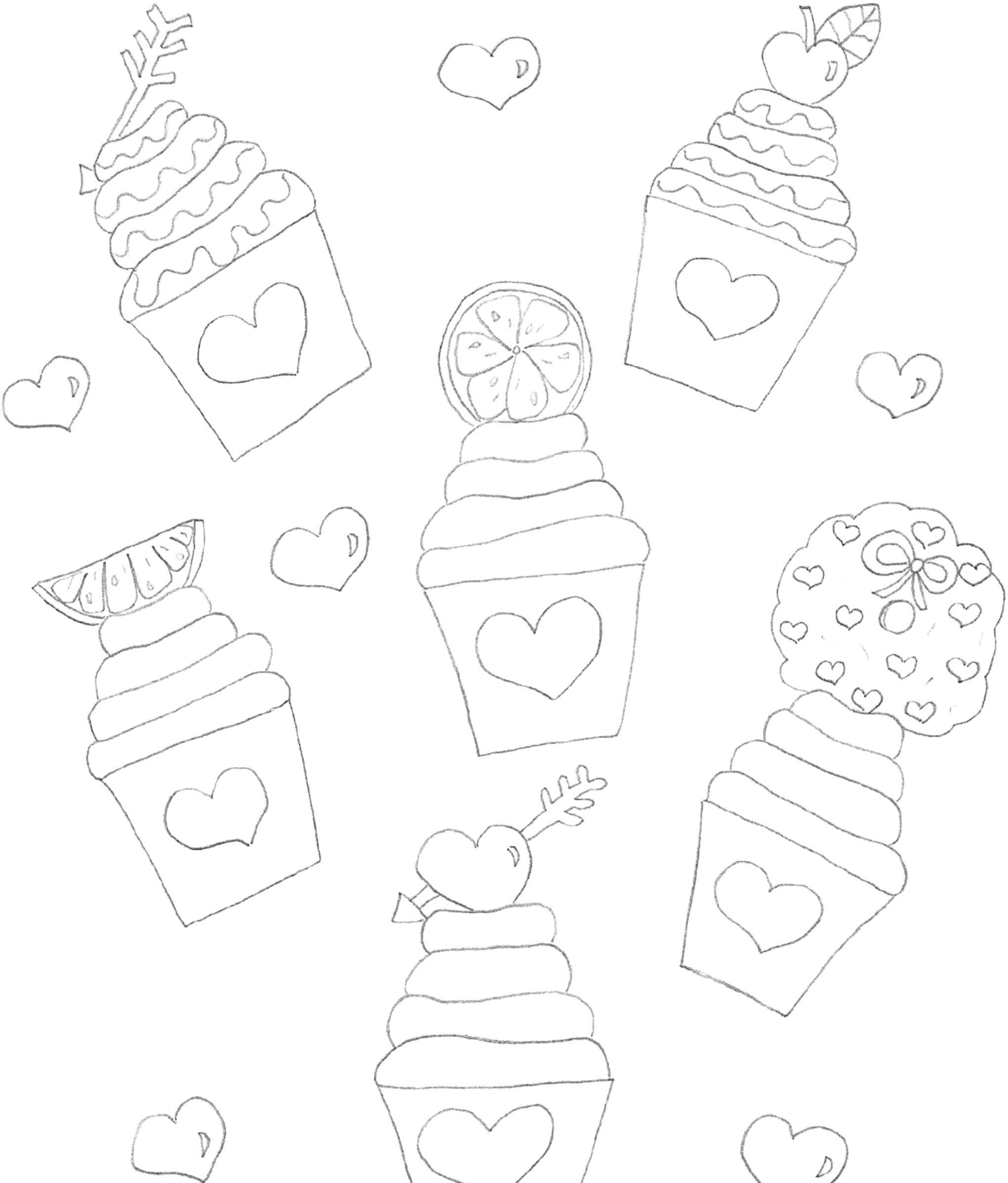

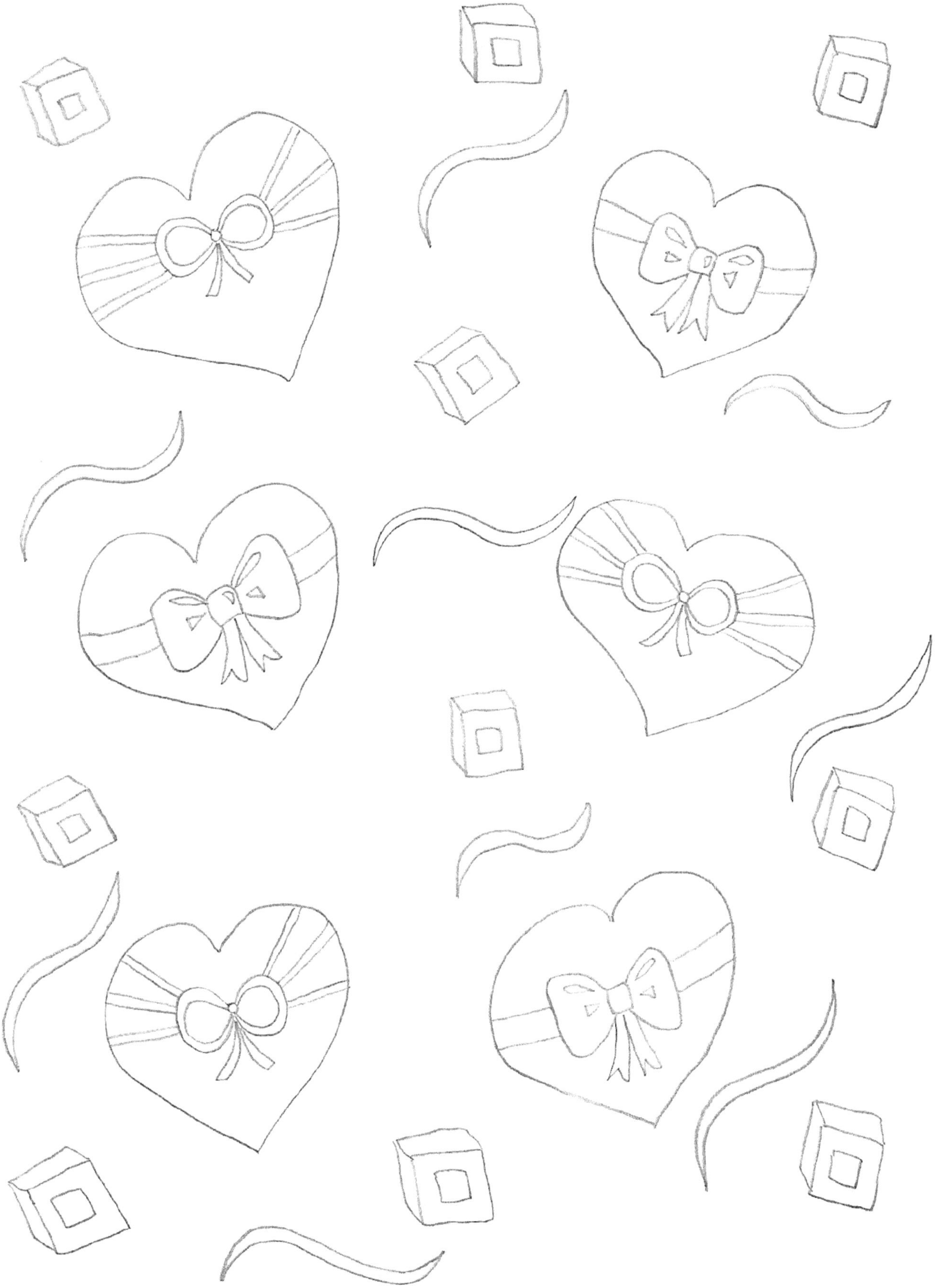

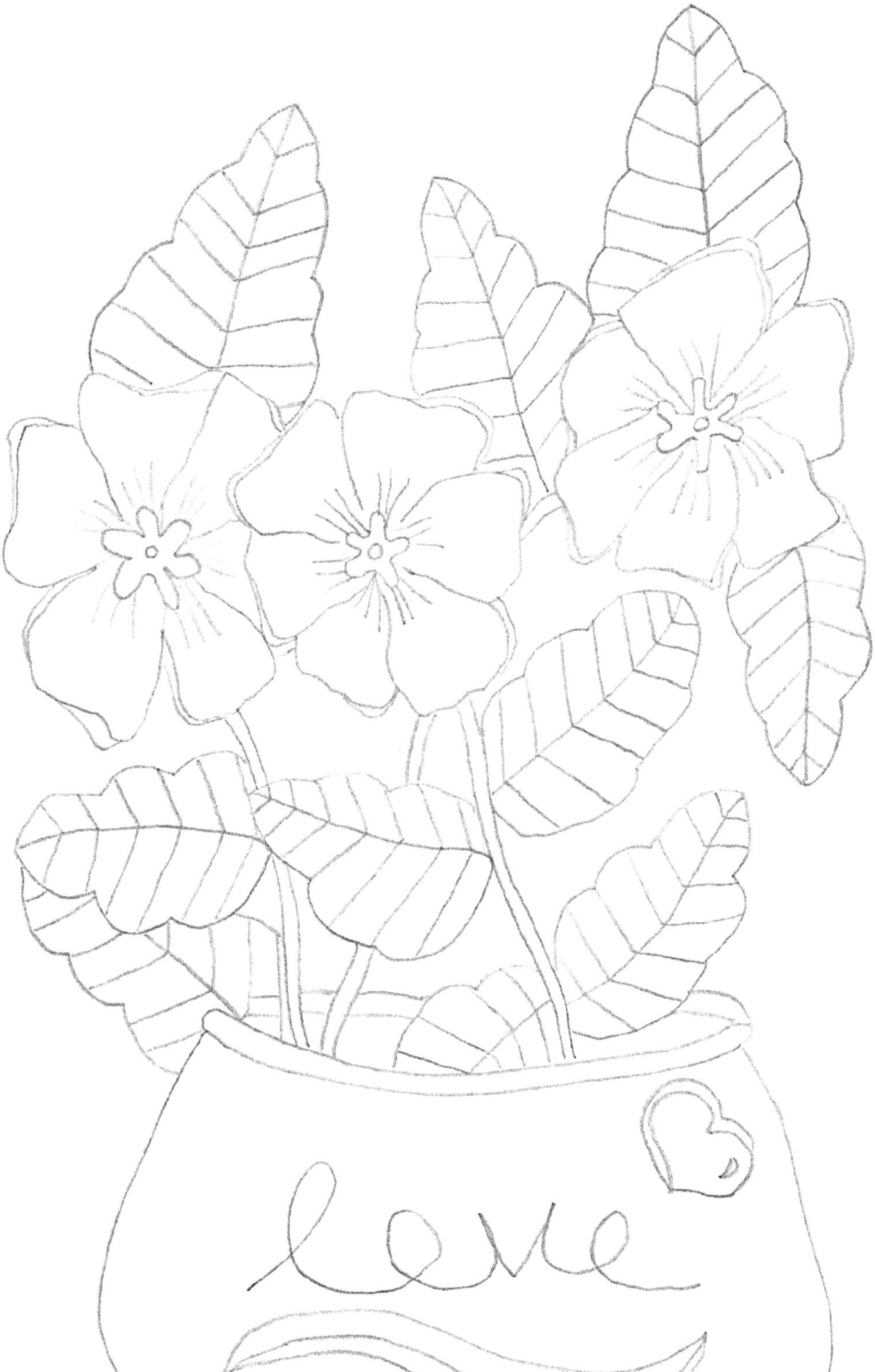
Love

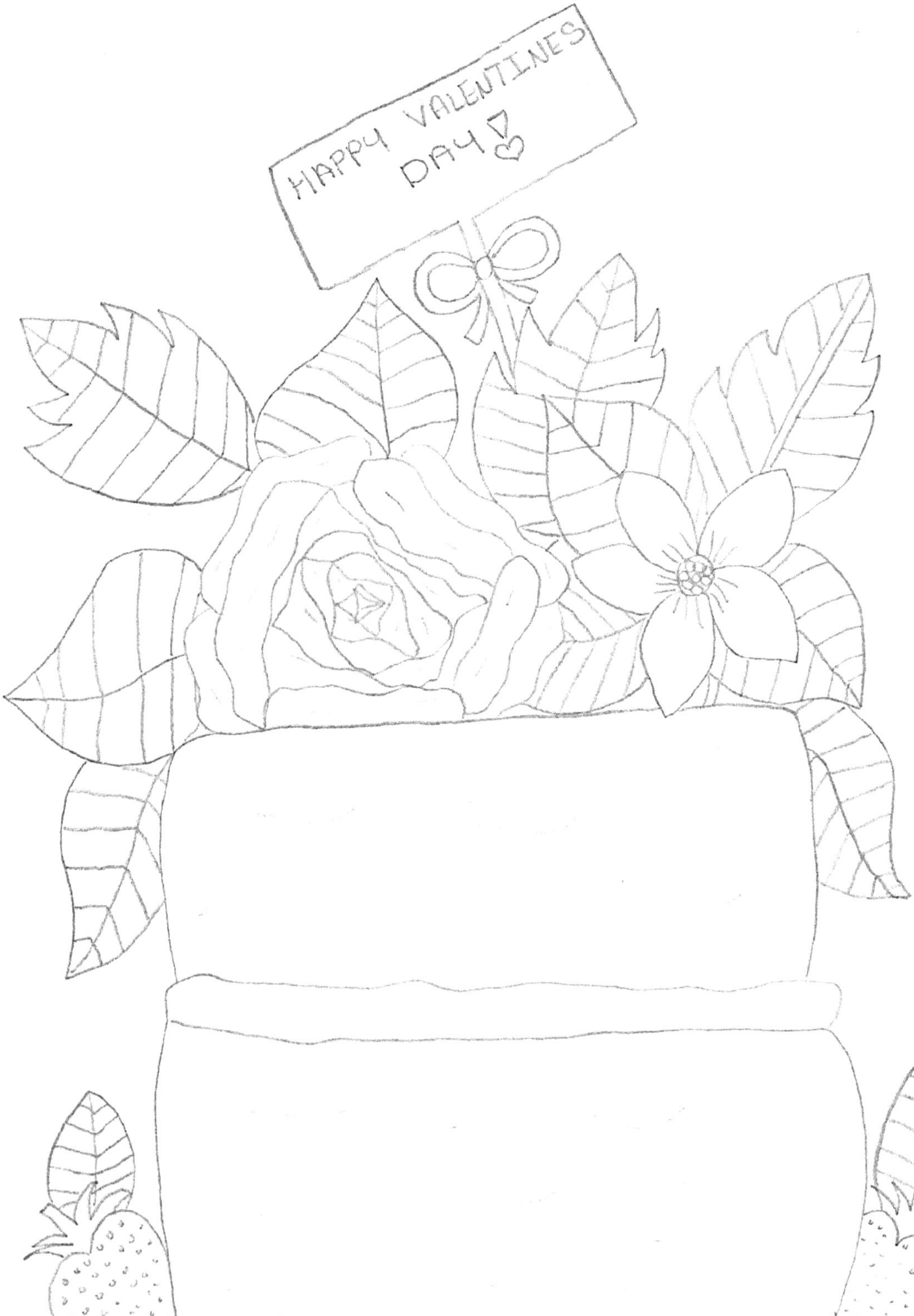
HAPPY VALENTINES DAY

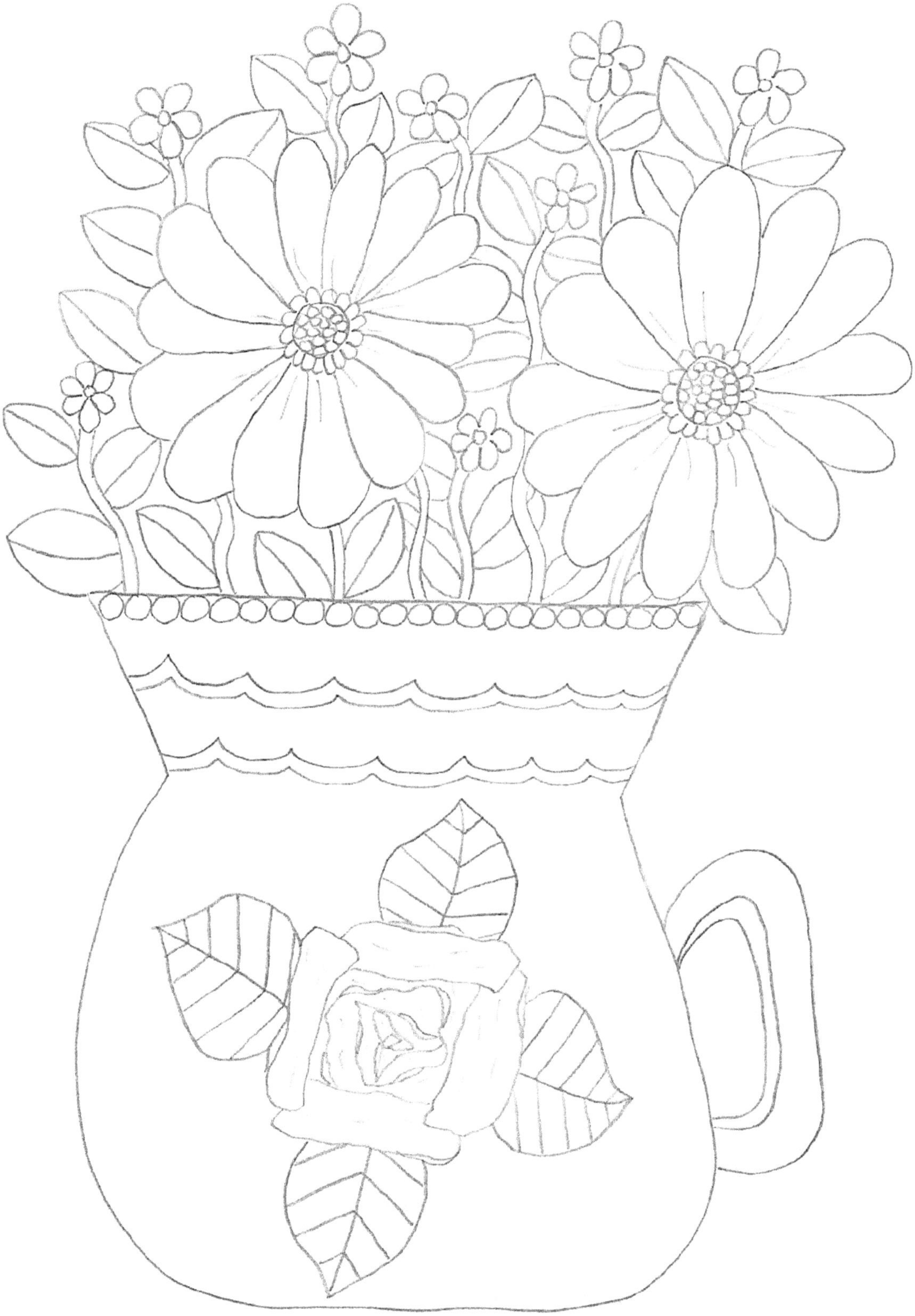

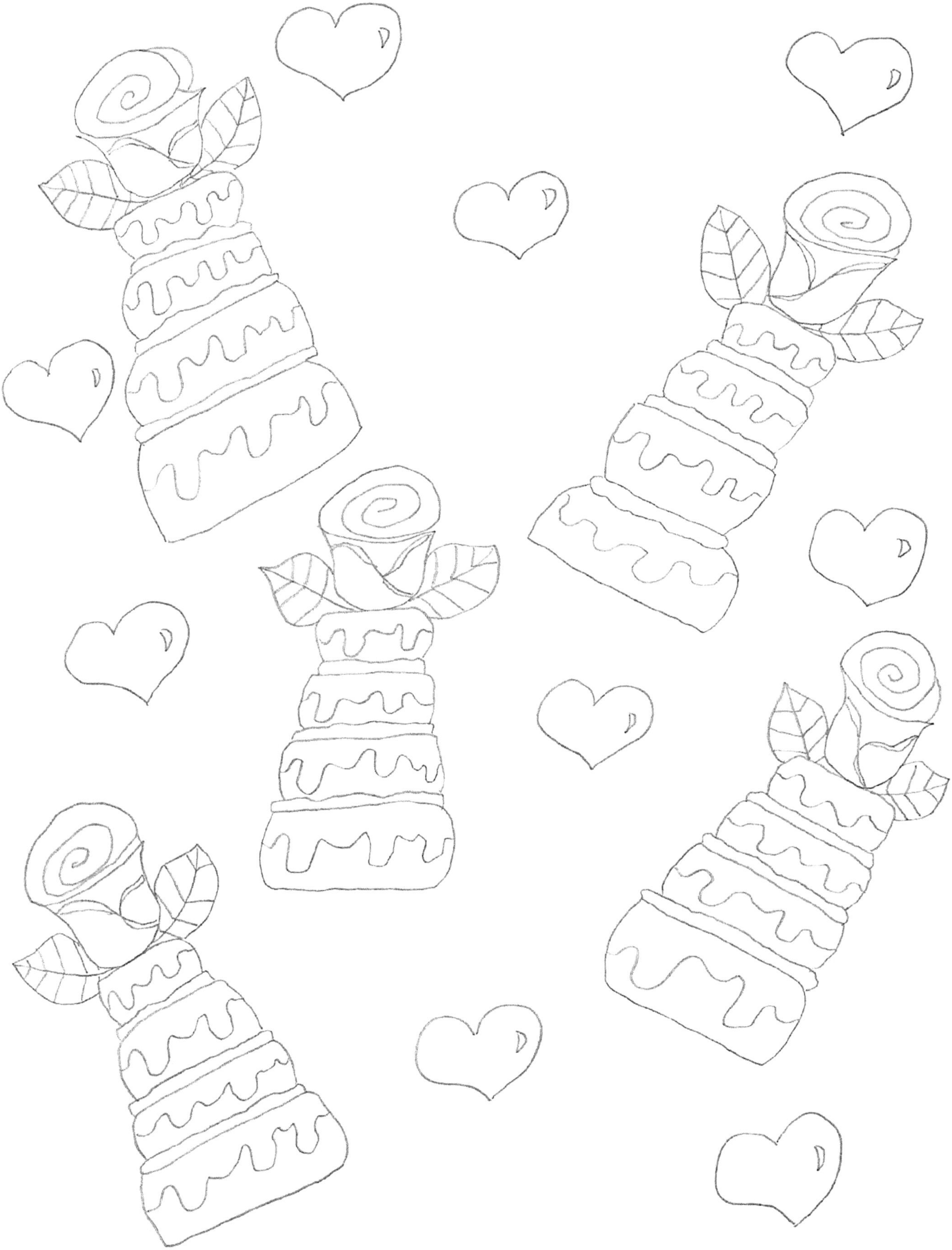

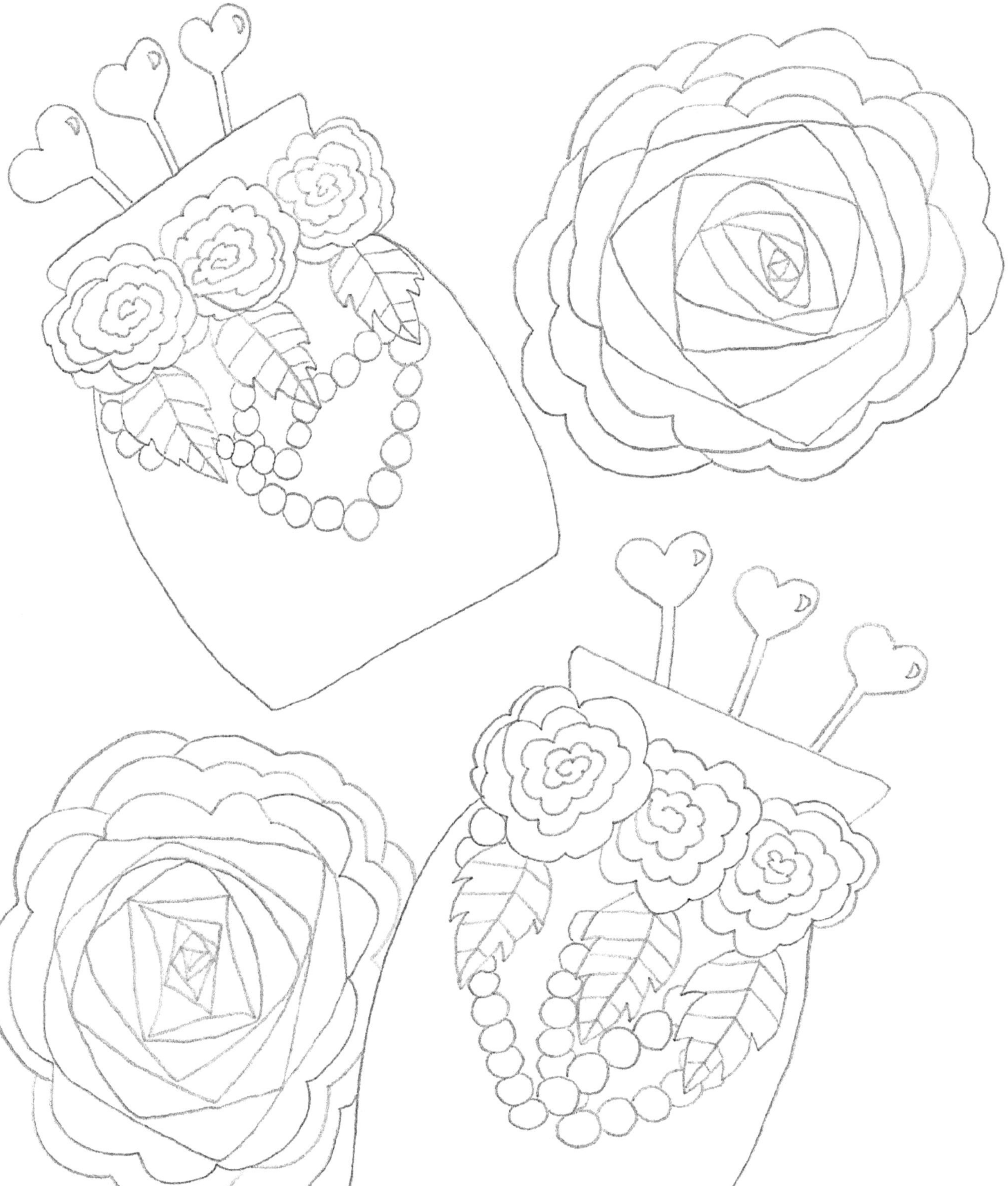

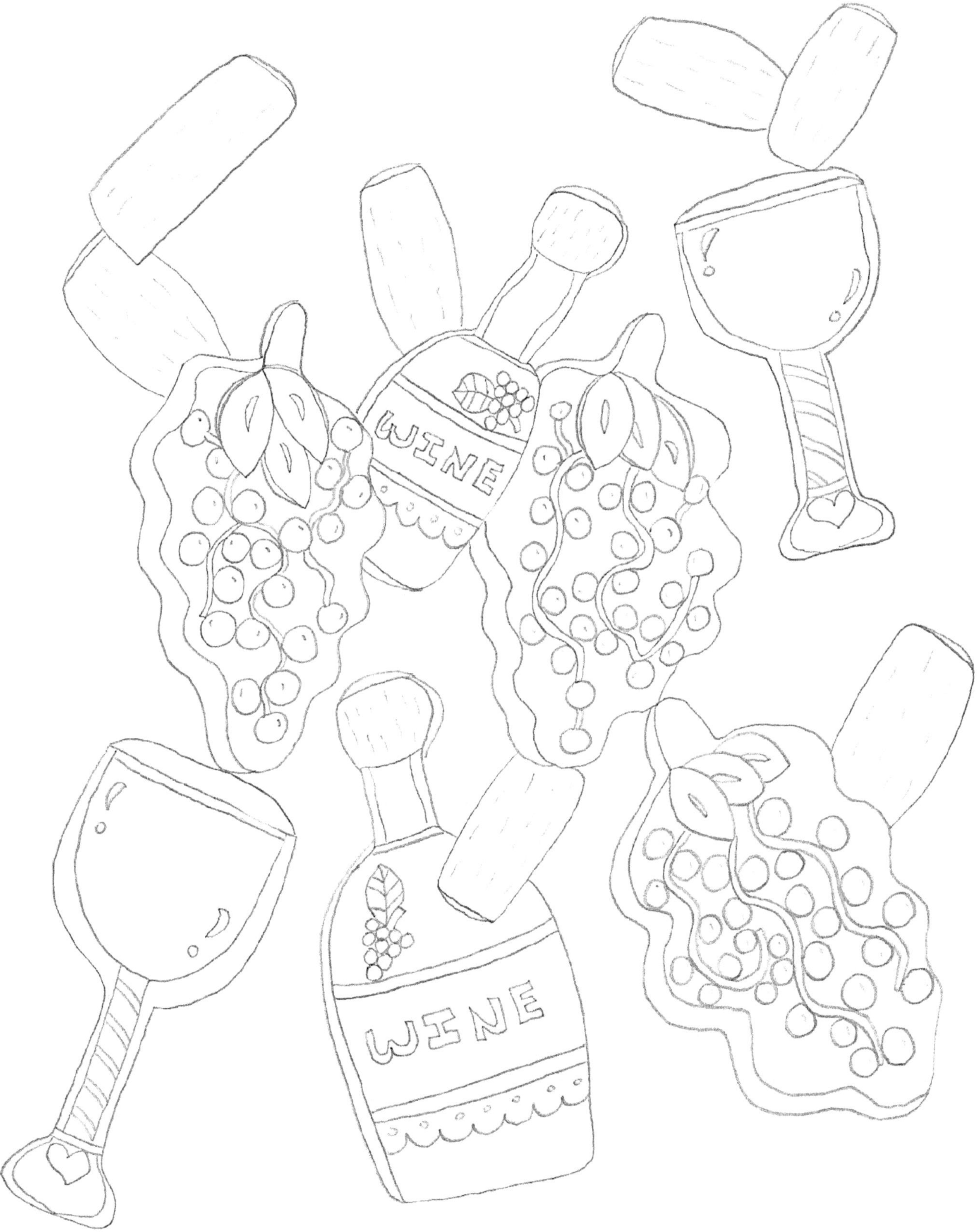
WINE
WINE

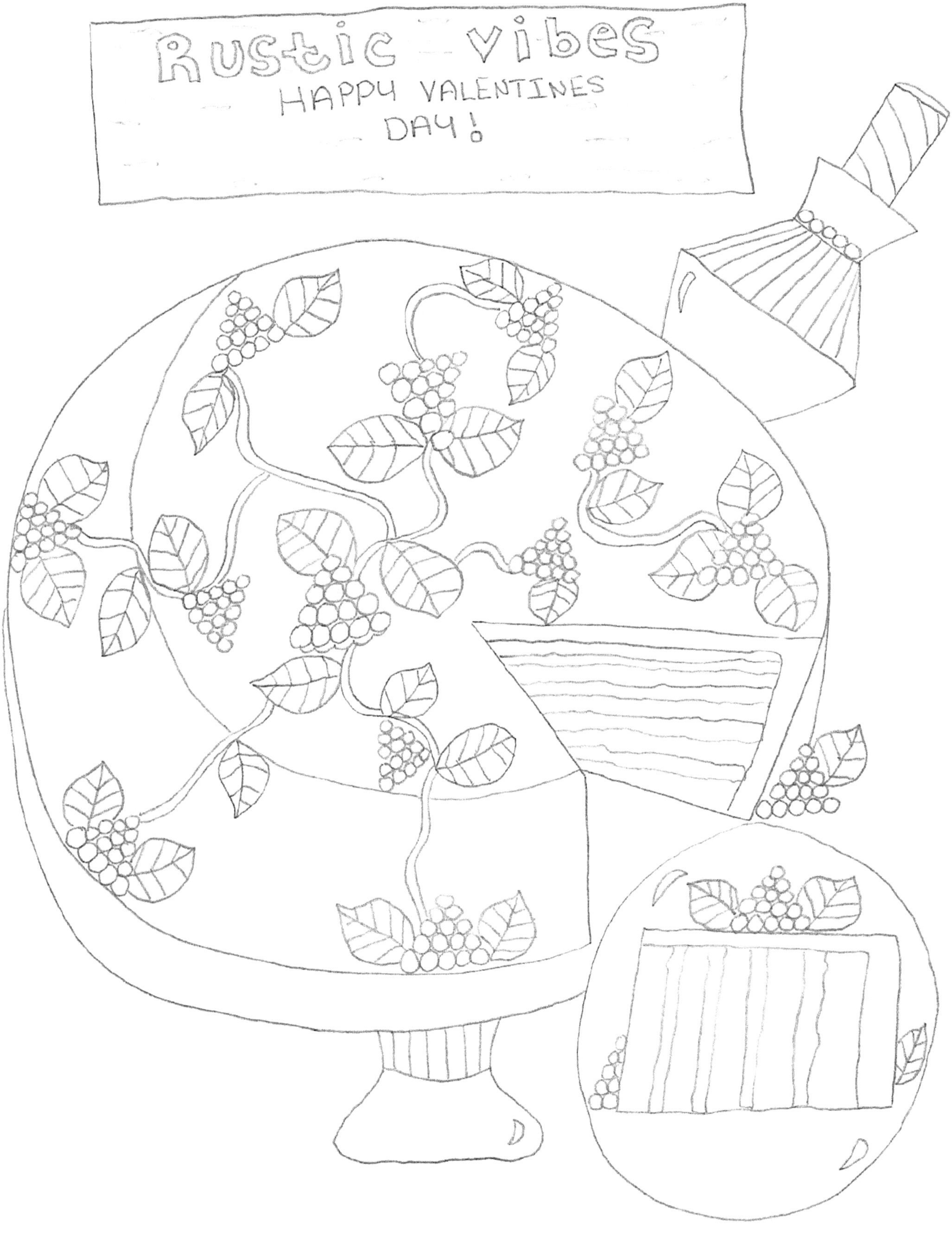
Rustic vibes
HAPPY VALENTINES
DAY!

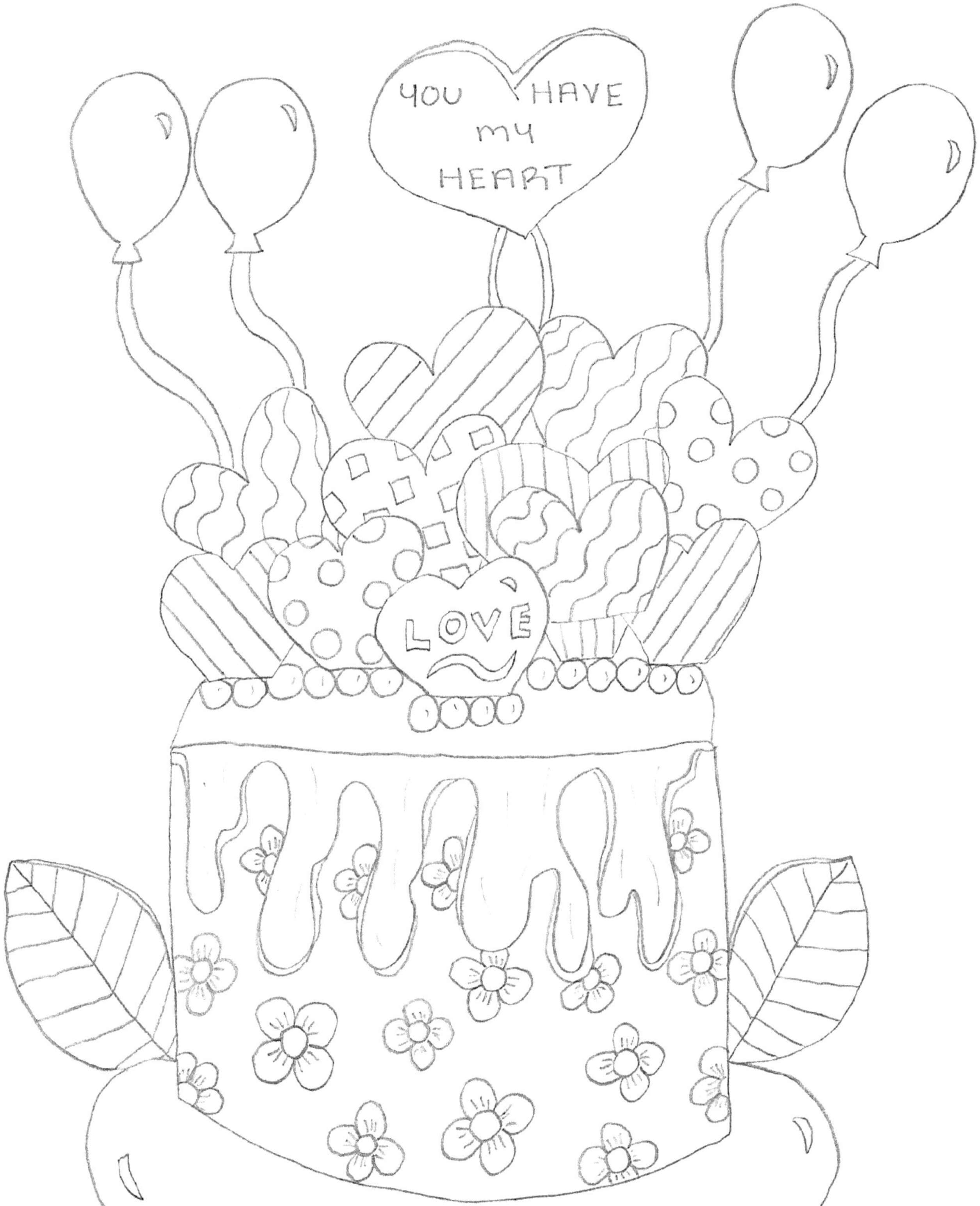
YOU HAVE my HEART
LOVE

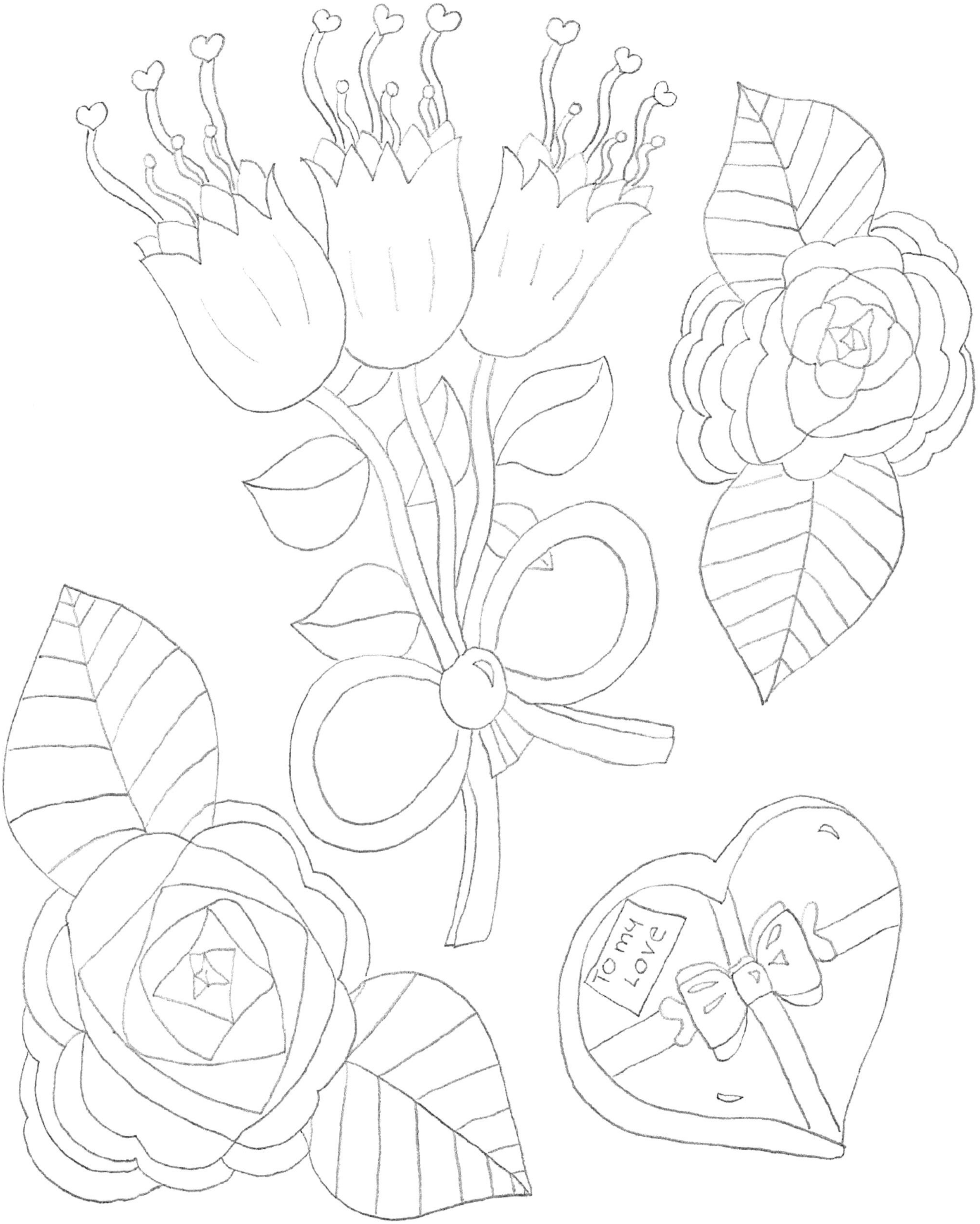
To my Love

XOXO
XOXO

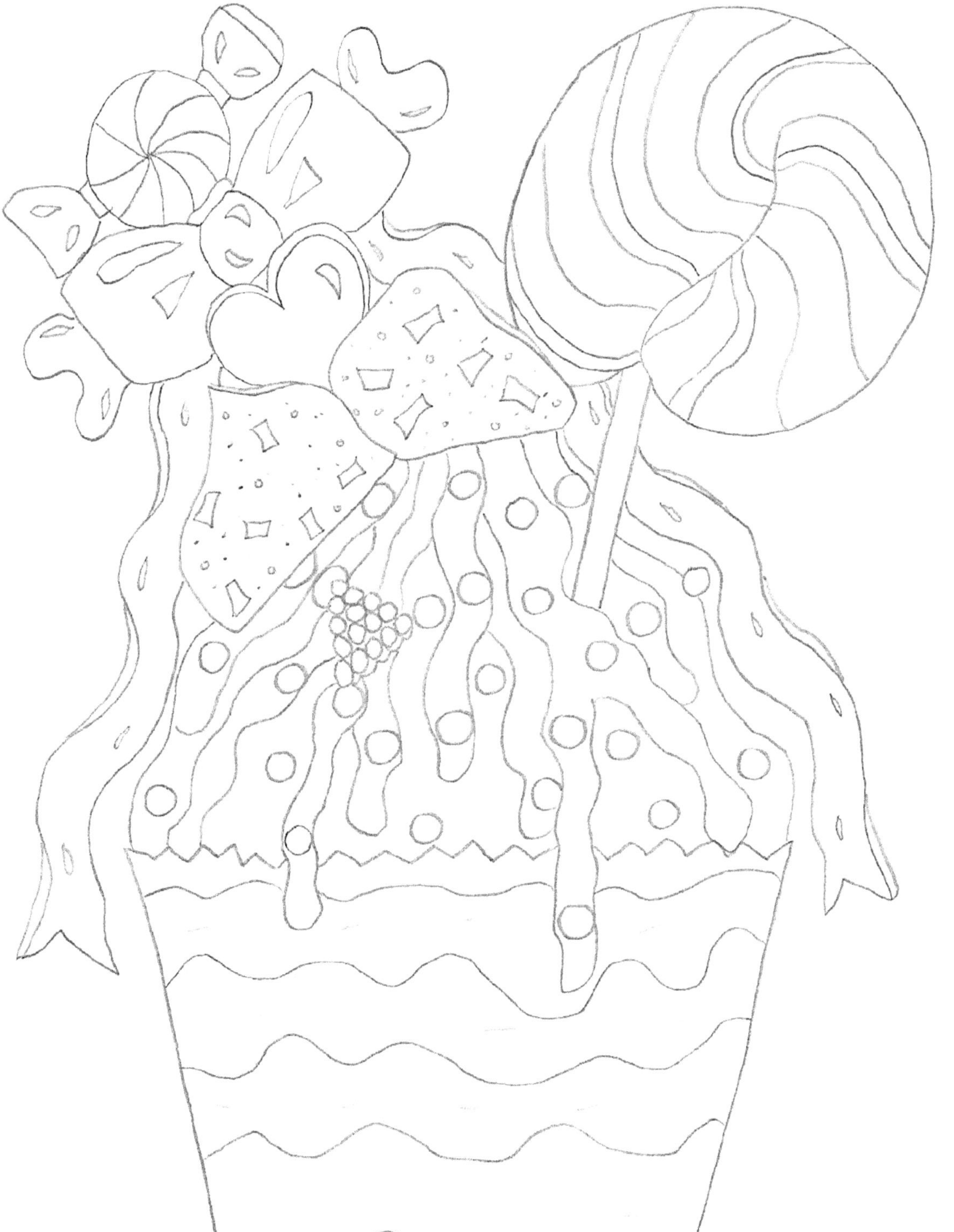

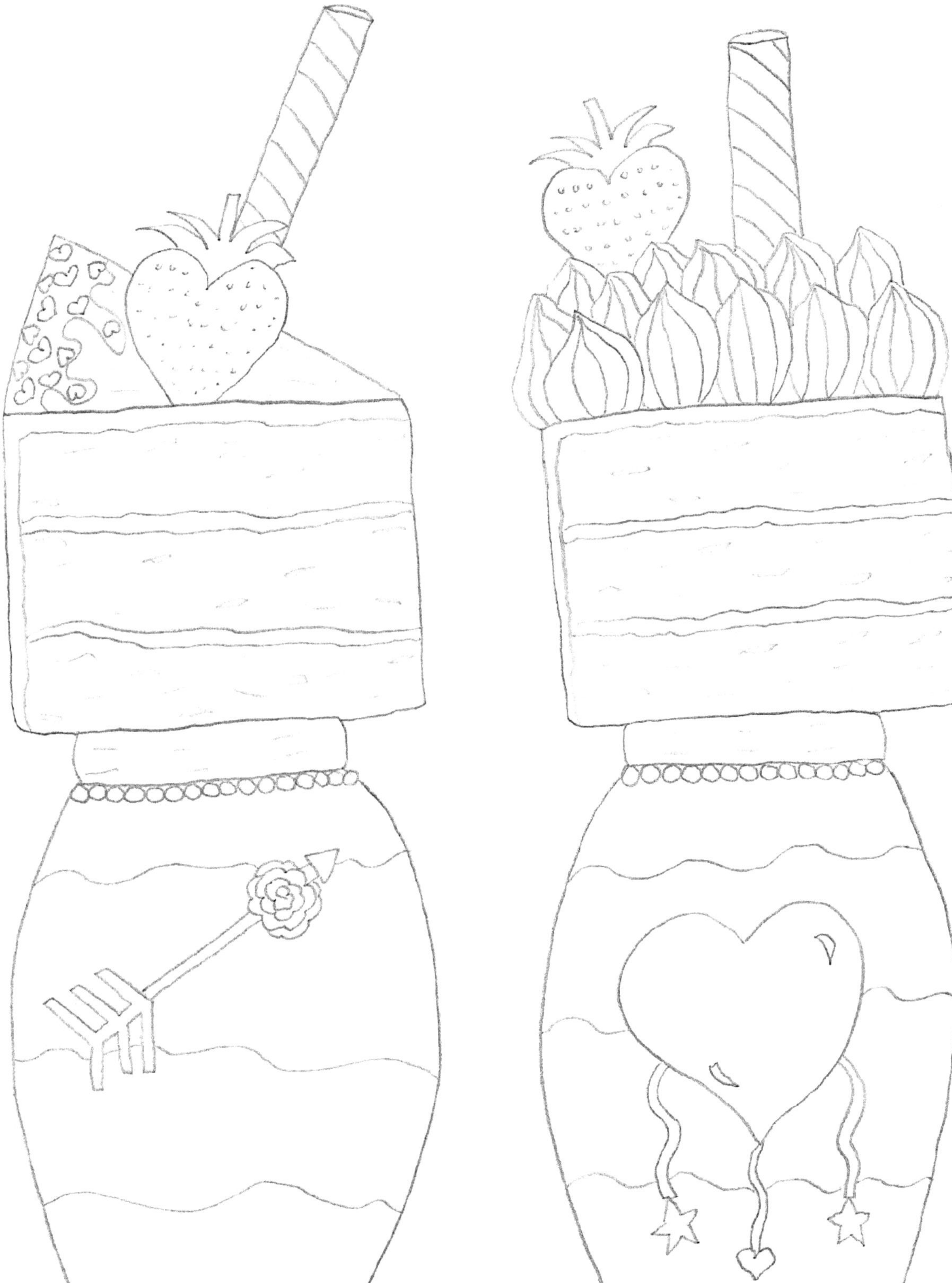

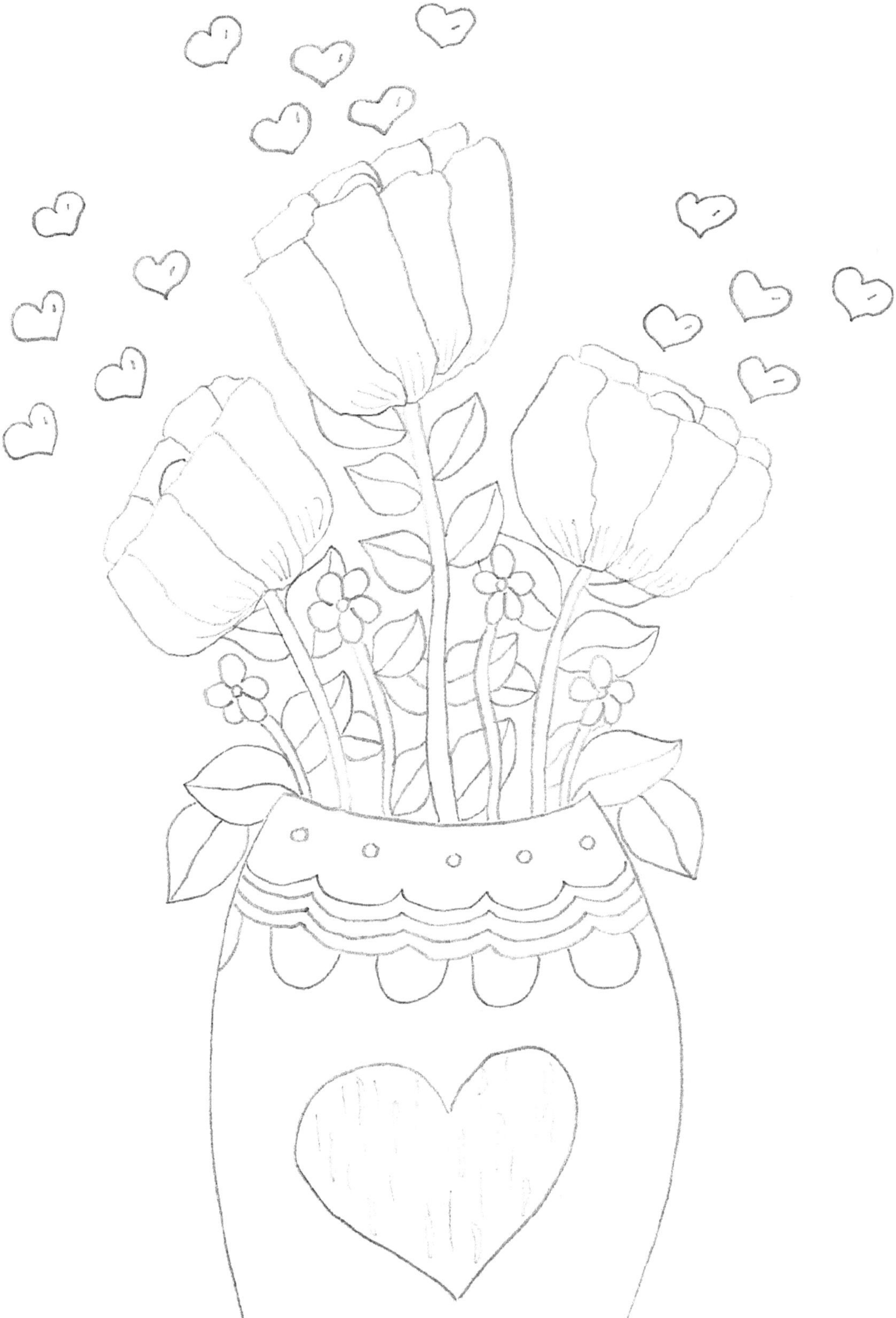

THANK YOU FOR PURCHASING A VERY RUSTIC VALENTINE'S DAY. YOU CAN CHECK OUT MY OTHER COLORING BOOKS LISTED BELOW WHICH CAN BE PURCHASED AT AMAZON.COM:

VINTAGE PARIS BAKE SHOP (Adult)

VINTAGE WINE GARDEN (Adult)

ICE CREAM MADNESS (Adult)

ICE CREAM MADNESS VOLUME 2 (Adult)

TEA & COFFEE TROPICAL TREASURES (Adult)

TEA & COFFEE OCEAN TREASURES (Adult)

TEA & COFFEE TREASURES (Adult)

BOTANICAL FLOWERS & MANDALAS (Adult)

MAJESTIC FALL (Adult)

A VERY RETRO CHRISTMAS (Adult)

MAGICAL DESSERTS (Children)

MAGICAL DESSERTS VOLUME 2 (Children)

MAGICAL DESSERTS VOLUME 3 (Children

FASHION DOLLS (Adult)

FAIRIES IN THE FLOWER GARDEN (Adult)

MERMAID'S WONDERLAND SEA OF ENCHANTMENT (Adult)

CHRISTMAS DESSERTS

VALENTINE'S DAYDREAMS COLORING BOOK (Adult)

VALENTINE'S DAY DELIGHTS (Adult)

VALENTINE'S FLOWERS & DESSERTS (Adult)

VALENTINE'S DAY DESSERTS (Adult)

VALENTINE'S DAY ANIMALS & Sweets (Children)

VALENTINE DAY'S FLOWERS (Adult)

IF YOU ENJOYED YOUR COLORING EXPERIENCE, PLEASE TELL OTHERS ABOUT IT BY WRITING A REVIEW ON AMAZON.COM UNDER THE BOOK YOU COLORED.

www.ingramcontent.com/pod-product-compliance
Lightning Source LLC
Chambersburg PA
CBHW081639220526
45468CB00009B/2493